Chapter One - How did we get here?

This is a question that I'm frequently asked, so here it is and to explain the title of "Accidental" as we have our plans and then life seems to alter this along the way.

Serenity Now Cottage (Seinfeld Reference)

Why am I showing you a before and after photo of Serenity Now Cottage? Well, this is the starting point. In 2010 I purchased the cottage which was a pale blue painted cedar boards. In 2016, after ripping out a water damaged outside deck, we decided to winterize the three season cottage into a year around property. What you will find out soon enough, is that I am frugal which does not mean "cheap" but rather means "value for your money".

Working closely with my friend and contractor, Paul, he was given the idea of salvaging the painted cedar boards. All the horizontal boards are reclaimed, as we carefully removed them and ran them through the table saw to rip the edge (of the blue paint) and flip them around to reveal the natural cedar wood. At $4 per foot (2016 material prices), you can calculate the cost savings in the thousands for doing all four walls of the cottage. The vertical tongue and groove cedar was purchased because we chose a four inch reveal on the lower overlap boards, which meant we had to buy materials. Because this is equity and investment, I chose to remove the old wood frame windows and replace them all with energy efficient, no maintenance vinyl. Spend money as an investment to earn equity in the value of the property each day going forward.

We shopped at ReStore, Goodwill, Salvation Army and ValuVillage before spending dollars at Home Depot, Lowe's, Rona and Home Hardware. If it was a specific item then we researched and bought it immediately (as time is money) but very often we find items online in various used item sites like Marketplace, VarageSale, Kijiji, etc. Lesson one - make a list, research options if possible and up-cycle whenever possible (helps the environment and keeping your expenses reasonable).

Paul got the idea for reversing the cedar boards from his friend, an architect that designed the Dragonfly Tiny House. The savings from his advice was in the tens of thousands of dollars. While we were winterizing and redoing the siding, Paul kept telling me how our efforts would give us an R value of 25-28 with everything we were doing, while the Dragonfly had R-40 walls and R-80 floor and ceiling using SIP Panel, interlock, construction technology. The most energy efficient materials, etc. He kept talking about the project of building the tiny house and how he was taking it to various home shows and jamboree's. The public response and fascination with tiny houses, was at a peak with all the home shows and downsizing trends.

We finished the winterizing and adding a sunroom renovation when we removed the outside deck that was water wrought and no longer safe to walk on. The project was a success and I invited the local real-estate maven out to take a look and give me her appraisal. What she said was surprising and quite frankly, amazing to hear how much equity we had gained (I'll go through the numbers in our Zoom Chats - my promise of transparency). While we were enjoying coffee, she remarked that I already had three out-buildings and the bylaw was that you could have four. She said if we built a small "guest cottage" and estimated $30k investment that the property value would be worth at least triple that when completed. Then she made the comment that changed everything...

"You know, if you rent out your guest cottage and show a revenue potential from a cottage property, then it would be worth five times or more based on the rental income". Regina Beach is a lakeside vacation community with a multitude of summer cottage properties - probably a 5:1 ratio of cottage to four season homes. Interesting idea.

Later that evening, with a beer and tape measure, I speculated on the possibility of rather than building to opt for buying the Dragonfly Tiny House (on wheels) and moving the trailer onto the property. Instant guest cottage without construction (actually, there was but I'll explain later). The Dragonfly was 8' x 20' and would fit perfectly - where it is located now - giving guests a view of the lake along with energy efficiency to keep operating costs low and most importantly, give people the "tiny house experience".

I'll digress for a brief moment - read the reviews since 2016 and you will see how many guests have enjoyed the experience of tiny home living.

Research - Research – Research

This should be its own chapter but I'll keep us moving forward in this preamble. The Tiny House was in a storage facility about 15 minute drive from the cottage. I would see it off the highway, every trip in and back from the city. Each time, it would get me thinking about how this might be a possibility. In my online research, I checked prices of building, adapting a shipping container, and all possible "tiny house" choices. I also checked the bylaws and building permitting process necessary. This project would require town council approval, as it would be the first STR (short-term rental property proposed in Regina Beach). Leading edge is also known as "bleeding edge" when you spend the time and money to pave the road for future developers with the same idea or copy-cat entrepreneurs who ride coattails, after the heavy lifting has been done by someone else. Keep that in mind.

First question - is it viable and will I get approvals necessary? Second question - can I get the Dragonfly for $30k budget of what we calculated the cost to construct a guest cottage would be?
Third question - could I convince my wife that this was a valid idea? This will be a separate chapter to answer.

Fourth question - What is my ROI (return on investment) - both in equity and from rental income potential? Run the numbers through Excel, which I will share with everyone including my cost analysis and ROI spreadsheet templates - happy to share with you, saving you time and money creating your own.

This was a chicken and the egg situation - do I negotiate and buy the tiny house first or get my approvals in place and then buy? I decided to negotiate the price first on condition of approvals, which was completely understandable, given we were on very new ground in this adventure. I arranged a meeting and we agreed on a price (I'll discuss all the details and numbers in future). Remember the idiom of "any money you save means your ROI is much quicker from revenue. Profit is derived not only from income but also from expenses you saved on paying out. Most people don't know this and few schools teach this - a lesson I learned in business very quickly and also a negotiating position to allow for flexibility and leverage. Another topic for a more involved discussion.

Next was the approval process. I talked with various people at the town office to get the breakdown on the process and timelines (estimates really), so we could have everything operational for the summer peak season of bookings and rental revenue. With my application to the town, I had to present to the town council for approval, meaning a vote from the three members. Two of them actually came to my place to see what I was proposing. The one member who didn't come to the property, asked the question - "my neighbour has a 5th wheel trailer - what is to stop him from doing an AirBnB like you're proposing here?" Good question. My response was simple. The town is in the business of increasing property tax revenue, so if your neighbour is required to tie in the electrical, water supply and septic, then it is no longer a "trailer" but now an "accessory building" on the property, subject to higher tax each year. The vote was 2 to 3 in favour. I was given the necessary permission to apply for a building permit. I should add, with the building permit an ad goes into the local paper and notification is made to the neighbourhood. There was one letter opposing the project - short story now, another person who wanted to buy the Dragonfly but her offer was rejected (low ball) and told to never return and waste their time. This neighbour had the same idea and was irked that I was going forward with what she felt, was her idea.

I delivered a cheque to purchase the tiny house. Arranged for Paul to get it from the storage yard and figure out how we were going to move it into position on the property. This is something many guests ask about and I'll cover in detail later.

We had to prepare the property first, which meant outlining where we needed to dig for underground electrical, water lines and septic tie in. We have a "call before you dig" utility service to find any underground lines we need to avoid. I'll discuss natural gas lines in more detail, as this was an "accidental bonus" and requires its own chapter. Everything was set. We had a plan and timeline of approximately two months, April and May, where the ground could be dug up (we have frozen ground over the winter months, making any construction project much more cumbersome and costly). My goal was to have the property ready for AirBnB (and VRBO, so from now on you know I mean both) by June 1st, 2016. My wife saw the tiny house when we were moving it onto the property with our Nest Camera. She called and we talked - more about this, as she has been instrumental in our success with her design vision that guests really appreciate.

This started the journey and next chapter we will go through the lessons learned and pitfalls. Before I end this chapter, I should mention, the Dragonfly Tiny House won awards at the Colorado Tiny House Jamboree for best design, and was featured on HGTV US and Canada. The host from HGTV US wrote the book, MicroLiving, which features the Dragonfly as a chapter in the book. Guests enjoy reading about the tiny house and experience all the improvements we did. We also set it up for year around with heated water lines, etc. but chose to close it down when we purchased the property next door (another chapter later) which is a winterized all-season home and we had "polar vortex" two years in a row that froze our heated water lines - this can happen at minus 40 degrees Celsius.

Thanks for joining and if you've read this far, next week it continues. Keep well. John

Chapter Two – Location, Location, Location and Research, Research, Research

Before starting your AirBnB business venture, I would advise to ask yourself and answer honestly, "do I want to be a host and share my space and do all the work necessary?" Most forget to ask this of themselves, and they find they are not "host ready", meaning they do not have the patience, tenacity or the ability to share their property with guests. In any service industry, the customer always comes first and (some readers may disagree) the credo, the customer is always right, is something some people cannot appreciate. Even when they are dead wrong, they are the customer and they are correct. The host must be patient, diplomatic and most of all, empathetic to see it from the customer's point of view.

It is one thing to research the numbers and read the success stories and it is another to peel back the layers and reveal the true cost – not just monetary but time and emotional toll. You are building a business and with it, there will be sacrifices. It is your investment and therefore, you are the person who will be required to "deal with" whatever comes up, as the decision maker, and owner. We will discuss delegation and building your support team in a later chapter – for now, please remember that each guest is a potential marketing agent for your AirBnB through "word-of-mouth" and this extends into the realm of social media marketing. Many guests don't stop at the AirBnB review but rather take pictures, post to their social media feeds, tell their friends, etc. Understand this and capitalize on your own "loyalty program" and create annually booked guests.

Let's talk location. In real estate this is a priority and it is shared with travel planners. Your location can determine; your value, your competition level, your success in bookings, etc. Is your location a "vacation destination" for people? This is where, if you are looking for your rental property, do the research and actually visit the location, talk to people, investigate online (essentially, research). Nothing beats "boots on the ground" and I always cringe when I read about people wanting to buy a rental property hours away from where they live. The added costs in time commuting as well as the stress of being an "absentee landlord" means you are multiplying your stress exponentially.

Each scenario is different and any time you spend researching can be equated to money you save on your purchase price – which means your ROI is reduced much quicker.

Research and location are intertwined and both are the priority in any rental property situation. We can look at different circumstances for vacation type locations but maybe you live in a University town and can rent to students or even better, visiting professors or parents. Each location will have its "pro's and con's", so making a list is crucial to having the facts in place to make a business decision. Don't be sold on "emotion" or "hype". Be methodical and pragmatic, do the list, do the math and visit the location many times during various times of day (old real estate trick if you watch the movie "Seven" you will know what I'm talking about during the dinner scene and the train rolling by every five minutes).

My story was simple – bought the cottage which is a thirty-minute drive from the city (unheard of in Toronto but common in Saskatchewan). Renovated over the years, learning by doing. Then the winterizing project and residing project took us onto the path of the guest cottage and what I described in the first chapter. I'll discuss the expansion into other properties, in separate chapters, as each deserves the time and consideration of the facts.

Research is part of planning and if you are buying anything that requires renovations – always factor in a contingency of at least thirty percent on costs and time (a lot of people forget that scheduling is important, especially if you are aiming for a seasonal peak rental location).

Talk to various realtors regarding the location. Look at the town bylaws, as some do not allow STR – case in point, look at recent laws imposed in Vancouver and other states in the US. Ignorance of the law is not a defence and not knowing can cost you dearly. As I said, every situation is different which is why I have consulted over the years with various want to be hosts and hosts looking to improve what they were doing. There are always options to consider and ancillary business and marketing opportunities if you know where to look and how to capitalize. If you can provide a service or product that nobody else is, then you can raise your exposure and in direct proportion, your profit margins and ROI.

AirBnB is now introducing new "comparison tools" which is great. Before this (soon to be released update) you would have to switch to travelling on your profile and do searches in your area to see what the rates are and how you compare. Where we are located, they are building a brand new six-unit motel, set to open summer of 2024. This shows a lot of potential where it will encourage tourists and visitors and is great for the town investment overall. This also provides a "spill over" option when you are booked solid and fielding various inquiries. In addition, you can gauge your rates and what you offer compared to theirs. We are not competing in the same market, as our customers are looking for a family friendly location to vacation and most importantly, we are pet friendly which I'm sure the motel will not be. I've recommended other places to guest inquiries that I couldn't accommodate and for this, both the guest has appreciated this and the proprietor of the business has, where I have received guests from their recommendations.

Part of my research tools is my spreadsheets (which I will provide to subscribers for free). There is one which covers fixed and variable costs to operate. There is one that forecasts ROI based on various levels of cost per night (and now per guest), at various percentages of occupancy over the year. This chart is great for creating "best and worst and median case" ROI expectations. There is also a renovation estimate and actual cost spreadsheet where I track my over/under budget line items. This has helped reduce costs and creating more realistic estimations when doing a renovation plan and budget.

I want to take some time to explain how you should rationalize your thinking around your expenditures and expenses. What I frequently do is equate this against how many nights rental income it would take to cover these expenses. Simply put, don't be penny wise and pound foolish as the saying goes. If your hot water heater is very, very old and will definitely need service or replacing, factor the expense against how much it would cost in refunds for guests not having hot water. Also, if you need to replace this then investigate purchase outright versus rental options. Every expense is a potential business operating cost write off, and therefore reduces your income tax exposure. There are many situations which dovetail into various branches and options or a "domino effect" where a decision affects other factors immediately and potentially in the future.

Contingency is not just for budgets but also for operating. Just like a cashier keeps a float amount in the till, any business should have a "petty cash fund" for anything that might come up. I also have contingency built in to my operations, like extra supplies on hand. Here is a time is money saving process I discovered and will share. If you have one set of sheets, towels, etc., that have to laundered in-between guests and you have a limited amount of time for all your cleaning requirements then invest in "one to show and one to go" idiom. What I have is three sets, so I can essentially leap frog on the changeovers. This way, there is no delay in laundry for setting up everything for the new guests arriving. This added to our start-up costs but each hour saved from having your cleaning person waiting for the dryer to finish before doing the bedding is saving you time which saves you money.

Buy quality for a number of reasons. Guests appreciate it and benefit from it. Materials will not breakdown sooner with repeated laundry and use. You save time on having to purchase replacements. The list goes on and if you go back to rationalizing against ROI on the number of rental nights, it makes complete sense. Also, if you upgrade your property, you set yourself apart from your competition while increasing the equity in your investment. Think of it as when you sell your property, it is now a "turnkey purchase" for the buyer, where everything is already set up from day one (they literally turn the key and they are in business).

My wife has decorated all our properties and she has created wonderful spaces that our guests appreciate and enjoy (and also respect the thoughtfulness and personal touches). We will discuss "theme decorating" in a later chapter along with purchasing options, as there are some things you can buy used and other items, for consistency and quality that you are advised to buy new.

I hope you are enjoying the information and finding value from it. If there is anything you would like me to discuss or questions you might have, please let me know.

Chapter Three – Negotiations, Budgets and Insurance

We're going to cover a lot of ground in this chapter and I'll try to post an audio version (and a video tutorial to cover the spreadsheets interactively).

Negotiations

Probably the best books to read on this are "How to Win Friends and Influence People" by Dale Carnegie, "The Seven Habits of Highly Effective People" by Stephen Covey and any book like "Getting to Yes" on negotiation skill building. I'm not a fan of "debate judo" or other such adversarial tactics when negotiating.

My takeaways in a nutshell – when talking on the phone, write down the person's name and always refer to them by their name during the conversation. Carnegie knew this was an excellent way to tear down barriers and put simply, it is true. Next, remember that your "emergency" may not be someone else's emergency (and vice versa, so keep this in mind when negotiating with guests). "No" is a perfectly acceptable answer and is nothing personal in business – the correlation is that if you answer "yes", then there is a commitment to complete the work or an obligation on your part. I always tell people, "no good deed goes unpunished" and this applies to saying yes and helping others when it will become your chore (most likely with a deadline attached making it "very important and urgent" when Covey says categorize every task "import, not urgent").

If you draw a triangle and put a symbol for time, money and quality at each point – your customer gets to choose two and you and the supplier/service provider keeps one. This little trick has had a profound effect on keeping everything balanced, as just like a table with two legs won't stand, you need the third working in conjunction to have a three-legged table. My printer taught me this and it has worked every time without fail. If your customer demands all three, then that is not a customer you want to do any work for, as they can't empathize and appreciate your time, your expenses or your quality of work.

Negotiations are always towards a "win/win" scenario. Anything else is doomed to have problems or someone feeling leveraged. Each situation is unique, so going through each possible transaction would be impossible as everything is nuanced. As in chess, there are so many possible moves and with each move of a piece on the board, the entire dynamic changes. Again, this is not an adversarial "win or lose" proposition, but rather just explaining that there are multiple options and domino effects from any decision on both sides.

If you are not knowledgeable about a subject, take the time to learn or speak to people who can guide you. This will save you time and money along with actually knowing "what" it is you are wanting or what is involved. Make sure everyone is on the same page and definitely, keep records in writing. This can be your notes from a phone call or meeting, getting quotes (and get multiple quotes), looking up project sequences and scheduling (like having gas installed you are dealing with the gas company and then a gas fitter that is you contract separately).

Keeping good relationships with your suppliers is also a factor of marketing as many situations arise where they offer your name and number as a contact to friends and family looking for accommodation. They also are a potential "reference" for other suppliers, so if you don't deal honourably then this may come back to bite you down the road, usually out of the blue and when you least expect it. If you live in a small community, it doesn't take much to spread, so be aware of what you say and to whom you are speaking (you never know who is someone's cousin and badmouthing someone is never advised).

Any project you undertake and any quote you receive, add your contingency – and this is a good point to segue into our next section.

Budgeting

Remember, you are operating a business. This means debits and credits or money going out as expenses and money coming in as revenue. There is another option for revenue, which is saving money on expenses (penny saved is a penny earned…) that many people forget to consider. If you save spending a thousand dollars because you took time to do research, then this is a thousand dollars less you need to earn in order to achieve your ROI. Simple concept but one that goes missed far too often.

Keep track of your fixed and variable expenses. Keep track of your income sources and complete your own "financial stress test". If you are spending more than you are earning, then you will soon be under water financially.

Knowing your financial position should be a priority so there are no surprises and you always should keep a contingency fund – call it a "building fund" or "rainy day fund". Whatever you call it, this amount is for emergency situations that don't financially stress your resources. With interest rates soaring, don't make the mistake of using a credit card to save you. This is fraught with interest rates that will put you further in debt that you will cause you grief or that you may never recover from.

Go to your bank and secure a HELOC or LOC (home equity line of credit or line of credit) that you can use as an operating line and pay back immediately from rental revenues.

Keep a monthly forecast income sheet which has a budgeted amount column and an actual amount column (and I add a percentage over or under column so I know for next time what amount I should be budgeting). I also have Break-Even ROI spreadsheets, so I can enter various scenarios to see what we need for pricing and income. I have these spreadsheet files and will provide them to my supporters, along with a tutorial on how to enter various rental rates based on a number of factors (amenities, number of guests and comparative rentals in your area, etc). This will be a video tutorial to go through the spreadsheets and creating real-time changes in your appraisal process for pricing.

It is much easier to teach by showing or doing than it is describing in text, so I'll leave this here for now and reference back to this when we do the video tutorial on this.

Insurance

Necessary expense to protect your investment. Does every insurance broker understand STR and how AirBnB and VRBO are the first insurers if a guest has an issue where a claim has to be made? Quick answer, "no". They don't care or don't appreciate the $2 million dollar insurance fund if you have guests that cause a major damage claim to your property. Keep in mind, it is not just the repair but the time it takes to fix that could delay accepting new guest reservations and therefore cost you rental revenue.

Any broker can go through the list of options on coverage and how this can affect the annual premium you will pay for insurance. Sometimes this is not disclosed fully, so making yourself knowledgeable and reading your policy, line item by line item is very important. I found that insurance underwriters are automatically charging for "identity theft coverage". This may seem trivial on the face, but in actual fact I pay for this in my banking fees, so if there ever was a breach, who would be paying, my bank or my insurance (or both)? Neither have been able to answer and yet, both charge a fee for this coverage.

If the insurance broker is using a "cookie cutter" or "boiler plate" policy (something they cut/copy/paste) then you may be paying for coverage that you will never claim. We had this at our condo where they were charging for a "shared equipment" such as a boiler or AC unit. Problem is, these are townhouse condominium complex and there is no shared equipment. Over $300 per year was being paid on equipment we didn't have and a simple phone call to remove this from the policy saves thousands every three years. Reducing expenses is a factor in revenue income, from saving paying out these fees. Whenever you have the opportunity to reduce costs, then your ROI timeline towards breakeven is also reduced.

In Canada, there are provincial insurance companies where they broker to larger companies that underwrite the policy. These companies, of which there are only a few, operate nationally. These companies also don't deal directly with individuals. For years, I've asked why AirBnB doesn't establish their own insurance brokerage firm to deal with the underwriting companies on behalf of their STR hosts. Maybe this isn't in their business model, yet they charge in their fees for the host insurance coverage and act as insurance appraisal "tribunals" when you as a host submit a claim. Maybe it is just too "easy" for how I am considering it and maybe I don't know enough to speak on behalf of AirBnB or VRBO. If they read this, maybe they want to at least appreciate, from the hosts perspective that this is a financial hurdle that we face annually (and with inflation, it is only getting more expensive on our operating costs).

Over the years, I've read countless questions on various group sites about this very topic. Depending on where you live, who you talk with, and a whole host of other factors (like having property security and alarm systems which may reduce your coverage premiums) it is one of those necessary steps in your ability to safely host your guests, knowing your investment is protected. Some other factors might be your relationship history with your broker and if you are claims free or not. Just like automobile insurance, there are number of factors that determine if you are in the eyes of the insurance company "a good risk or not". Location is also a major factor in how your insurance may be calculated from the risk perspective. Is your property in a flood prone area or perhaps a fire risk area? Everything is considered by the insurance company so my final advice is to make sure you have a property appraisal, and inventory appraisal along with documents and evidence in the event any claim has to be submitted (before and after type pictures with date and time stamp on your files).

We will have a discussion on this, maybe even a Zoom livecast and invite a few insurance brokers to speak on behalf of how hosts can get the best value for their coverage. At this point, I will leave you and we'll pick it up on our next chapter. Keep well.

Chapter Four – Shock and Awe (Government Regulation)

This chapter will be specific to Canada but is applicable in some US States as well. I will keep this "apolitical" and deal with the facts of the current situation.

Research & Location (reprise)

Everything old is new again and everything goes in cycles. There is a lot of discussion about a pending "real estate realignment" in 2024. I don't have a crystal ball on the future. The crash of 2008 should have taught people something about how accumulated debt by the Government is shouldered, invariably, by the middle-class. We've seen the erosion over the years and if you haven't heard the phrase from politicians "in the future, you will own nothing and be happy with that" (and eat crickets, most likely).

In Canada the government is announcing an attack on STR and MTR in favour of their immigration policy and the lack of housing. As a solution, in the more desirable cities, they are imposing a rule that STR's may no longer claim any expenses as deductions on their income tax. Hmmm. Think about it. Question posted the other day by an STR Host in a major city – "How does that work, as I have over ten properties and a registered LLC (limited liability corporation). This is my business. Are they saying that a business in this particular sector cannot claim expenses? How is this fair?"

The government is there to collect the taxes but not offer any legal means to claim the expenses as a business. Keep in mind (just like in the States) you have three tiers of compliance; Federal, Provincial and municipal governance to comply with. This is where research and location come up again. You have to research the laws and bylaws on both the municipal and provincial first and deal with the federal laws later. Many cities are outright banning STR's to force property investors to sell or rent long-term. With the way the "rental tribunals" are set up in most cities, investors are given the "short end" all the time (speaking from experience with Ontario and it was a Gong Show from start to finish – save it for a rant one day to vent).

My best advice is to find a location, that has what travelers are wanting but there is not a lot of options for them. Stay away from larger cities, which on the plus side, the real-estate should be much lower in cost to purchase (therefore your ROI and BEP is quicker). You will also have more luck speaking with a local councilmember to argue the benefits of STR in building tourism to the local community and small business owners.

In my personal experience and location, they are constructing a six-unit motel (open in summer 2024) alongside a two-unit motel next door. You could view this as competition, but I do not. They are catering to a different traveller than we are. In fact, if I have a request but am fully booked, I will send them the links to book at other establishments (and other AirBnB's in the area). This is not only good business but in actual fact, their rates for what they are offer compared to our properties, proves our guests are getting much more for their dollar.

With all the tumult in the world right now and the adage that "real estate is the best hedge against inflation", we should talk about the cyclical nature of the markets. Property values will gain and lose, just like any investment. With the rise of interest rates, anyone who purchased on a tight margin of income will be forced to sell to get out from under the crushing debt load by even a 1% increase. That is how close some people are, even with the "debt service calculations" or the financial "stress test" banks are doing with mortgage applications. When a bank says "no" there is always a broker nearby willing to lend money, at a much higher rate. Let's face it, if you default, you lose your investment and your property. If your property is devalued in the market (which it was in 2008) then most people can't qualify to refinance and are forced to walk away with nothing.

Perspective is Important

The markets will do what the markets will do. Fact of life and of business. If you have made a good investment, then you have to keep your perspective and not be influenced by external factors. If you've done everything correctly, then you should not be forced into any situation that you are not in control of. Having said this, you've done your work, increased the equity in the property from when you purchased and have an income stream that is not only covering expenses but providing you with passive income.

With the aging population, many retired people are looking for PRI (passive retirement income) and an STR may be an option for many. Think about this, the market is down so selling your property to retire comes at a loss (and don't get me started on "reverse mortgages" = predatory lender that will take your property for half the value). You can be certain the market will improve in the future. If you can rent a portion of your home, then it offsets your expenses and therefore reduces the value you paid for your property.

Let's look at an example and keep the numbers simple. If you purchased a property for $200,000 and you can rent it out for $20,000 per year, then effectively after 10 years, the principal amount on the property has been paid. Each you can do this, means you have reduced the cost of the property overall. Add this possibility of you investing each year only 2% of the total value (so $4,000 out of your $20,000) into upgrades on the property, then you are building equity annually. Keeping it simple, if your investment is valued at $10,000 then the value of the property is increasing each time you invest. So, at the end of a five-year period you reduced the principal amount by half to $100,000 and you've increased the equity by $50,000 from your original purchase price. If the market value has increased by even 3.5% per year, then that is another $7,000 annually or $35,000 over the five years. Let's total this up now with the numbers (and keep in mind this is at a very conservative almost cost of living percentage market increase in valuation – some larger markets may see double digit increases) – your revenue has reduced the principle by $80,000 and you have increased equity of $85,000 ($50k plus $35k), so $165,000 ROI. If you sell for $335,000 then you essentially net close to $300,000 on your investment.

If any of the factors change, that is where your spreadsheet and market research come in to play. Imagine a 10% increase in property value over five years. Things can look pretty good. Even if you have a negative one year, the other four years will most certainly make up for any loss of value (and you have the rental income). This is not a "get rich quick" but rather a build equity, offset costs and generate your passive retirement income stream.

Work Smarter, Not Harder

Self-explanatory but often overlooked. I personally like reading manuals and figuring things out. Just the way I am. In figuring things out, I like to build templates for repeatable tasks that essentially creates a franchise model of operations. Take the time to learn how to automate your responses to guests with AirBnB with their "scheduled standard communications" option. I did this before with creating Notes, where I would cut/copy/paste my standard information and customize it to the guest. Read posts from other hosts that offers you a wealth of information and you can post questions directly to a group. If you're like me, you like watching YouTube "hack the world" videos, where people have ingenious methods of solving everyday problems.

Another way to reduce your time on your breakeven point (BEP) is by choosing a mortgage that allows you to pay up to 15% per year on the principal amount. This effectively reduces the principal and therefore the interest you pay on the amortization amount. You can also choose accelerated payments and weekly rapid. What this means is if you budgeted $1,000 per month in mortgage then pay $250 each week instead of the lump sum. Each day early that you reduce the principal amount means money saved in interest payments. Over years, this could mean tens of thousands of dollars saved and your mortgage paid in full completely.

In Canada, we have CMHC (Canada Mortgage and Housing Corporation) which is an office of the government that collects a premium if you are putting less than 20% down payment on your purchase. Essentially, this is an insurance premium payment to protect the lender from you defaulting. Depending on the purchase amount, this could be double digit thousands of dollars. Wouldn't you rather $15,000 go towards your principal amount rather than paying the banks' insurance premiums for them? Save your money and get the proper down payment to avoid paying this. Even if you borrow from a line of credit that you can pay down fairly quickly with revenues, then you will recoup this money instead of it being lost to the government coffers. Would the bank pay your car insurance if you were borrowing money to buy a car? No! So why should you pay their insurance.

Frugal is word that gets a bad rap. People think it means "cheap" when it actually means, "value for your money". Same with insurance premiums, property taxes, utilities costs, etc. There is no shame in asking questions if you don't know. Become educated and in some cases, as this has happened many times, even the person I'm speaking with had to ask someone else to get an answer – some cases they learned and shared a money or time saving method or maybe a loophole you can take advantage of. This happened when I asked about the property taxes and when they were due. As it happens, mine were due December 31st of that year but if you paid early by June 30th, then you saved 10%. With three properties, that was a $1,000 savings annually and if paid towards my principal, reduces my interest paid on my mortgage over the amortization period of many thousands of dollars. Domino effect in your favour if you take the time to do the research, plan and execute accordingly. Use iCal as a reminder on payments. Set up direct debit payments so it is automatic. Make sure you keep a contingency amount in your account and some have overdraft protection to eliminate NSF fees. Keep the minimum bank balance to avoid monthly banking fees. If you are senior, as about senior discounts. Some offer seniors at age 60 and some at 55, so ask and take advantage of these.

What I did for a few years was load a spending tracking app on my phone (now my banking app has this incorporated as part of their "value add" for their clientele). Chart on a spreadsheet for fixed monthly and variable monthly expenses to determine "your monthly nut" or your breakeven point. If your income is above this amount, then you are in the "black" as they say. If however your income is below this amount, then you are in the "red" and have to do some investigating. This should also be part of your process when purchasing a property. Just like you have a home inspection done, and conditions on finance, etc. you should receive all of last years utility costs, repairs, etc.

My Standard Operating Procedure for Home Automation

This should be its own chapter and may expand on this in an audio podcast. Here's how it works. Every property gets a: Nest Yale Lock, Nest Learning Thermostat, Nest Temperature Sensors, Nest Fire/Smoke/CO2 Detector, Nest Doorbell Camera and a Nest Exterior Camera. The Nest Lock is programmed with the last four digits of the guests' cell phone and programmed from their arrival date and time unit their checkout date and time. I add a contingency of time in case they forget something on checkout or arrive earlier (so from 12 noon on check in at 3pm and 12 noon on checkout of 11am). If you need a service repair person, you can schedule them access as well as your cleaning person. Saves money and time on keeping track of keys or missing keys. Also saves on your time having to go to the property. Is also a soon to be new feature on AirBnB with Smart Lock Integration on the App that will notify the guest of a specific code. You can also send your guest a "tap and go" option to have a virtual key on their phone to automate open and closing the door.

Nest learning thermostat and temperature sensors – a must for many automated reasons but most importantly, Eco temperature setting that lowers your heating when your property is vacant. This cost savings over the years will pay for the investment and you have increased the equity in the property with this upgraded system. You can also look at this expenditure as "one night rental income" and it pays for itself. We were able (even though Nest Support doesn't help with this) to connect the Nest Thermostat to control a gas fireplace as our main heat source, saving thousands over the years from using electrical baseboard heating. The baseboards are still in place and still functioning, as this is my backup if there was ever a fault with the fireplace not working. I did also buy an automated controller for the baseboards, so I can control this remotely as well.

By automating this, you have saved yourself time and money, as everything is remote from your phone, tablet or laptop from anywhere in the world. Couple this with temperature sensors (we have very cold winters and frozen pipes are a reality) and you can track your temperatures under the sink in the kitchen, downstairs by your hot water heater and in your bathroom (where you have water supply pipes). If the temperature drops below a set temperature, then you are notified and can address the issue.

***Before I forget, mention that you have this to your insurance company and in most cases, it will reduce the amount of your annual premium. Money saved, is money earned.

Nest Detectors are great and I always get the wired version, not the battery so you don't have any maintenance requirements. There is an internal battery if there is a power failure, so it has redundancy built-in. This is also great for detecting people smoking in the property. We allow smoking outside the property but not inside. We also have a Ion Air Generator that we purchased primarily for the tiny house and Airstream from cooking smells, but works great in any property to eliminate odours in any room from carpets, couches, and mattresses. I'll provide more information and links on these (and they are not sponsors, so there is no paid endorsements here).

Nest Doorbell and exterior camera is perfect to monitor your property to know when your guests arrive but also to see if there is a "more guests than booked" arriving. If you have a no party policy or you are charging on a per guest basis, or have a no pets policy, etc. then this allows you to monitor and record footage that becomes your evidence if you ever have to message the guest or consult with AirBnB Support Team. You are not "spying" on your guests, you are monitoring your property to insure your investment is not being "mistreated" and your house rules are being complied with. Again, the insurance company likes this home monitoring automation and is a type of "security system" self-monitored. Nest does have a monitored home security system but it is not yet available in Canada.

Summary on Automation and Technology

Technology is great when it works. Keep on top of monitoring and make it part of your daily routine with your coffee in the morning. This can help you manage your property from anywhere. Case in point, it happened that I was admitted to hospital for a kidney stone. That same day, my phone goes off and someone has booked my place, same day arrival. From the emergency waiting room I was able to use my Notes file for the automated message communications (cut/copy/paste) and then program the lock code and schedule check-in and checkout dates and times and set the temperature so the place was comfortable for their arrival. I was also able to have my neighbour bake a pie for my guests as a thank you for booking gift (opened and locked the door remotely for my neighbour when she was at the door with the pie – Nest Doorbell Camera).

That weekend I slept at the hospital while the guests enjoyed the property. My cleaning person also has a door lock code of her own, and was able to access the property after the guests checked out for the cleaning and preparations for the next guests.

My properties have septic tanks that require a truck to pump us out when full. I did try automating a water sensor for the septic tank level. This worked the first time but started having issues. Just so you know, I went back to my trusty float and stick septic level indicator. It is not automated and I have to check this at all properties but it is accurate and always works. There are more expensive systems on the market and I may revisit this in the future. I should also mention my Septic service company is great. All I do is text them and they schedule me in with date and time (so I can let guests know in advance if necessary) and it is paid on my credit card on file and they email me the invoice for my records. Template the system where it is seamless and saves you time and money and hassles.

Let me know if you have any questions or would like a particular topic covered. Thanks again for reading and keep well.

Chapter Five – Setting Up Your AirBnB Rental

Tailor The Experience

You have your property and now you are planning repairs and renovations before you do your set up and staging. Always keep in mind that this is a rental property for guests. This is not about your like and dislikes but rather what the guest is needing and wanting for their vacation rental. As I said before, you can get value for your money and evaluate the existing furniture (if any) along with the bathroom and kitchen. If everything is very clean and well kept, then hire a cleaning crew to come in and bring everything to showroom condition. If not, then make a list of items you need to change and proceed.

In my experience, I've sold the kitchen appliances and bought used but in great condition, many times much less than the tax amount on a new appliance purchase. This is especially true if the appliances are mismatched in colour scheme. If you don't have the time and money then clean and repair what you have, run your rentals for a year and save up enough money to upgrade at a later date. If you apply my rule of calculating how many nights rental it would cost to recoup your expenses, then you may well be ahead of the curve. Also, this provides you with the time to source used replacements to upgrade with, saving you on the purchase price (and "frugal" getting value for your dollar).

The bathroom is an interesting room, and should be well thought out. If it doesn't have an exhaust fan, get one installed. It is very easy for mold and mildew to inhabit the space and may require some remediation work on your part. On the good side, it is most like the smallest room in the home to renovate if you have to replace the wall material (it may be drywall, particle board, plywood, etc). Make sure you replace with mould resistant drywall so you don't have to worry about this in future and you have increased the equity in the property. Make sure to keep your receipts and take pictures, especially if you replace the 2x4's with mould resistant blue-wood (treated product) that will be hidden when the walls go back up.

If you do have the walls open, this is the perfect opportunity to make sure the walls are properly insulated. This is not only for the exterior walls but also for the interior walls with sound insulation batt material. This accomplishes a few things; sound insulation, heat transfer reduction and again, increasing your equity (make sure you take pictures and create a "build book" that you can show before and after shots).

The bedrooms should have at least one master that sleeps two people comfortably, along with the other bedroom or bedrooms. What we have found is using bunk beds in the spare bedrooms, single over full size mattresses, means that potentially with a three bedroom you can comfortably accommodate six guests. Quick formula being used to calculate rental rates is $50 - $75 per guest, per night. This may change with your research and when the comparison tools become available on AirBnB soon. Make sure the rooms are comfortable, have sufficient lighting, perhaps a bench or chair for luggage and maybe even a desk area for doing work.

We specifically use laminate flooring for many reasons. Low cost and maintenance being the most prevalent. This is also easy to clean with a quick brush and then using a mop. To save time on the living room area, we have a Roomba iRobot vacuum that we turn on before proceeding to stripping the beds and doing the laundry.

Same Day Guest Check Out and New Guest Arrival

We have a four-hour window between check out time and check in time on a same day turnaround. We talked before about "creating a system or template" and this is important in saving time in between guests. Also, saving time on cleaning means you are not paying out as much on the cleaning fees on a per hour basis. If you are doing your own cleaning, then you will appreciate these next few chapters.

Purchase multiple sets of bathroom towels, bedding sheets, and kitchen towels, bath mats, etc. It is far easier to remove used towels and sheets and replace immediately with a clean set. For this reason, we have three sets of towels, sheets and replacements so if for any reason the laundry can't be done, you have two changeovers before needing this done. This also helps you keep track of your numbers for supplies, as we count all our full, hand and face towels in our changeover sets. Also, we colour code our sheets for queen, full and single so it is easy to know which is for what room. Also, if you don't know how to tell the orientation of a fitted sheet, the label will always be at the foot of the bed on the right-hand side. Anywhere you can reduce time in between, you can save hours which equates to hundreds and perhaps thousands of dollars in cleaning fees.

Also, we should mention that the flooring choice allows us to provide a "pet friendly" accommodation. With the ease of cleaning and protective laminate, we can offer our guests what most motels and hotels won't allow. We provide pet bowls, litter boxes, pooper scoop bags and even doggie treats. We also charge an additional fee, and if necessary, can go towards the additional cleaning time required, and in some cases (we own our own carpet steam cleaner) to steam clean the carpet and furniture. We have also purchased an Ionization Generator that can clean the air of impurities and smells, which is great for these types of situations.

What separates your property from the competition? What can you provide that your competition cannot? If a guest has to board their dog, then the cost can mean hundreds of dollars extra without the company of their furry family member. By offering an affordable solution, guests are happy to pay the few dollars extra to have their pet(s) with them. This might not be possible for your rental situation (some condo complexes have bylaws against pets) but if it is, then you should really think about this.

Cleaning Supplies

Many guests are frustrated by having to pay cleaning fees and now being tasked with a "cleaning checklist" before they leave your property. Many have said, if I am cleaning up then why am I paying a cleaning fee? Fair point and needs consideration. One strategy is to reduce the cleaning fee and add in the cost on your daily rate. This seems to work in most cases, as it could come down to two properties and yours has the lower rate for cleaning.

Make sure you have plenty of supplies (paper and plastics); toilet paper, paper towel, kitchen wipes, kitchen catcher trash bags and large trash bags, blue bags for recycling, etc. If you are going to leave instructions, as we do, for what we expect on check out, make sure it is reasonable and doesn't crossover into what they expect the cleaning person to provide. All we ask is that trash is put in outside containers along with recycling (which we donate to a local pet charity) and the used towels are placed in the bathtub. The rest, we take care of including, having guests load the dishwasher only. We have enough plates and cutlery that they shouldn't have to run the dishwasher (unless they are booked for longer than a week).

In the kitchen we also provide paper plates and plastic cutlery, as many people prefer this when doing a BBQ outside. Speaking of BBQ's, we have installed direct natural gas lines to save on propane tanks and refilling. If you must have propane, always make sure you provide a backup bottle that is full in case your guests run out. You may even want to invest in a propane gauge that can be checked and swapped out if necessary. I'll repeat myself here again, installing a natural gas line increases the value of the property and the convenience of saving time and money running to the gas station or hardware store every time you run low. The natural gas line factors all this redundancy so you reduce your maintenance costs and recoup the benefits over time.

For coffee, we provide a Keurig coffee maker, a drip coffee maker, a kettle, toaster, toaster oven, microwave oven and an assortment of teas, sugar, sweetener and coffee whitener. Guests know in advance to bring their own Keurig coffee pucks or drip coffee (we have either paper or reusable metal filters). Make sure you have a good assortment of pots and pans and lids. For the microwave, provide a plastic shield to prevent excessive time cleaning splatters. You can use shelf paper for the cupboards to protect the cabinetry. Try to use a countertop material that is easy to clean and low maintenance. Tile is not just decorative but is functional protection for the walls in the kitchen and easier to clean. Make sure you have a good cutting board(s) so your countertop is not damaged.

Bedroom Extras

For each bed we like to use memory foam mattresses. If you already have mattresses then consider a memory foam mattress topper. We also install a mattress protective fitted cover that not only protects the mattress (investment) but also is green tea infused and waterproof for any accidents. If you are pet friendly, then definitely this low-cost investment will protect your mattress investment by only having to wash the fitted mattress protector. This is also about guest comfort and our way of competing with higher end hotel beds. We also purchase new pillows for the rooms, as old pillows lose their shape and comfort over time.

We have heard of some guests replacing pillows with old ones and although this has not happened to us, is something we are aware of and watch out for. By discussing this with your cleaning person, they can take a picture, make you aware and send the customer along with the picture and note that this was not the pillow you provided for their stay and will be replacing it with a "money request" for the cost and time. The host can even take a sharpie and put a distinctive symbol on the corner of the pillow, and for that matter, all the bedding. Hotels do this with embroidered sheets, towels and even shower robes. Believe me, if any of these are missing, the guest can certainly expect an additional charge on their credit card.

Keep track of your inventory and as simple as this sounds, if you set up your system properly, then you will reduce these types of situations. As a final note, when you communicate with guests make sure you are diplomatic in your note about any missing items. People can become easily offended and retaliate with a negative review. We'll discuss this in detail in an audio podcast, as I've been asked how you deal with this particular type of situation and retaliatory guests.

Living Room Extras

In the living room, make sure the furniture is comfortable and well placed that it defines the space for your guests. What we have done is installed electrical wall outlets that have USB charge ports built in to the receptacle. It is your choice to provide the charging cables but I suggest not, only because there are proprietary ports and connectors to each phone and you do not want the blame for damaging a guests' phone.

In the living room, we mount the TV on the wall with an articulating mount so the guest can angle the view. We also subscribe to a few streaming services and use our WiFi system instead of paying for cable or satellite. We have found the Amazon FireTV 4K Stick to be the most cost effective peripheral device for this, along with Prime TV, Prime Music (and you get free shipping on all your orders as a Prime Member) and Netflix along with free streaming apps like Tubi. We also have a Google Home Mini, which provides music, weather information, can be set as an alarm clock, timer, etc. Try to limit the clutter of alarm clocks and specific use items.

Books, Games and Activities

In the living room we have a selection of books, games and activities. These we get at garage sales and asking people, if they don't sell by the end of the day if they call you, you'd be willing to return and collect them (sometimes pay a lump sum). The books we provide with a donation box for the local pet charity, so guests can take the book and leave a donation. We've had this and some guests really appreciate this little gesture that they don't feel guilty for not finishing a book and taking it with them. Creates a nice thing for your guests while providing a win/win for the local charity.

For games, make sure they do not contain little pieces that could be a child choking hazard. It is for this reason we don't put Cribbage boards with the tiny pegs in our games. We also make sure if we have a puzzle that the pieces are of a sufficiently good size to reduce this risk. We encourage everyone reading this to consider what might be a potential hazard and limit the risk and ultimately the overall liability. Guests have appreciated these personal touches and our consideration for their safety. It is not just children but also pets that can potentially chew on items that could cause a problem.

Defining an Overall "Theme" in Your Decorating and Design

My wife does all our interior and exterior decorating at all our properties. She is personally responsible for outfitting all the used purchases, dollar store purchases, bedding, towels, etc. Her philosophy of style is figure out the "theme" along with the colour scheme for the property and maintain a consistency throughout. She has also brought this into what decorations are put on the wall, be they coat and key hooks to paintings or open shelves. We always have a white board that either goes on the wall or with a magnet on the fridge.

All the furniture is "form and function" with captain's bed, functional as a bed and dresser drawers for storage. Space saving and multi-functional and multi-purpose when possible. Again, guests appreciate the attention to detail in a space that is functional, stylish and comfortable.

Laundry, Laundry, Laundry

This question seems to come up quite a bit on the various discussion groups. We only provide laundry for guests staying over a week. Our laundry facility is separate from the living area, so they require our permission and the door unlocked to access. Providing the guests with a laundry bag and have them pack it for you to throw in, shouldn't be a problem (especially if they are extended booking guests, and many might be return, ie loyal, annually returning guests).

We are lucky in that we have a laundromat close by as well, not only for guests but in the even our washer or dryer is in need of repair or replacement. This is a Plan B, for redundancy, as breakdowns will always happen when you are at your busiest.

I've read posts where guests have abused the privilege of the host providing access to laundry by doing excessive amounts at the property. In our case, this would fill the septic tank very quickly, which is why we don't offer this and also ask guests not to run the dishwasher, as this too can be excessive and fill the septic tank rather quickly. This adds to your expenses along with the water supply, electricity to run the dryer and the laundry soap and dryer sheets. It all adds up when you provide this. Also, factor that this is particular equipment you need for your business and "lending" it to a guest who doesn't know how to operate it, could be a recipe for a breakdown.

Each situation requires its own review and analysis to figure out a solution that is win/win. I'll leave this hear for an interactive Q&A style podcast so we can brainstorm various scenarios with actual problem solving from the group. Maybe there is something we can learn and put in place for our guests that works better than what we are currently doing.

Thanks again for reading and keep well.

Chapter Six – Social Media Marketing – The Good, The Bad and The Ugly

Preface of Marketing Principles

Any Host that relies one-hundred percent on just their AirBnB listing to draw in prospective guests is not living in the reality of the market. Having a listing on VRBO also aggregates to about fifty or so other sites, like hotels.com, Travelocity.com, etc and because of this, there are two middle-men payment percentages, which is why VRBO guests often pay a higher booking rate. Hosts have to understand that the listing is not the defacto only way to reach guests.

Understanding and using Social Media Marketing to their advantage, is how hosts are able to target local populations more likely to visit within the area just a short distance from their residence. These are more commonly phrased "Staycations". A confluence of factors caused the rise in reduced travel for vacations (due to Covid lockdowns) added to the inflation rates on energy pricing which hit the airlines and subsequently costs passed down to the traveler. If you are traveling on business, then no problem as it is not coming out of your pocket. For many others looking to vacation in their normal, pre-pandemic climate, this just wasn't possible.

Instead of seeing a decline in AirBnB guest bookings, there was actually a sharp increase. We can see that these are starting to decline back to pre-pandemic levels. Hosts should consider that they make themselves aware of not just the competition but other societal factors that are occurring in their markets that illustrate as "peaks and troughs" on demand. Simple things like an event or concert will drive up demand over a specific time period and something a host should pay attention to and monitor.

AirBnB Pricing Algorithm (Smart Pricing or Dumb Pricing?)

The "set it and forget it" of Smart Pricing employs a type of AI that is supposed to be doing comparative analysis in your local market of how many vacancies are remaining and at what price to reflect on your rates. In my personal experience, sometimes this works well and other times, it inflates the prices to an unrealistic amount for the reality of what guests are willing to pay. Case in point, when I had dynamic pricing on to try it out, it tripled my rate but there was really no justification in a comparative analysis. Maybe I was overthinking this problem but in the off season, many three season cottages are shut down over winter thereby reducing competition on the platform. With a limited number of listings coming up on a search, the Smart Pricing increased substantially, effectively pricing us out of the reality of the market.

This might be the "The Bad", where you should be getting bookings but potential guests are put-off by the higher than hotel rates being listed. Personally, I turned off the Smart Pricing feature and decided to, especially for the off-season rates, enter my own comparative rates with a little price comparison research. Not scientific or highly quantifiable but what I would expect to see as a guests searching for local accommodations. Having the history in the area to have seen the rates develop over the years gives me a little more insight than any AI algorithm just crunching numbers.

Some hosts may disagree and have seen amazing results from Smart Pricing. The only occurrence I can cite where this did work, was when there was a musical festival locally, with very high demand and low vacancy availability. In this one case our tiny house rented for about four times the normal rate over a week. Other than that, we have seen a decline in the bookings due to a number of factors, one of which is the dreaded off-season.

I should explain that the off-season of winter, still has a lot of activities and events which should see bookings. Depending on the year, word-of-mouth, the activities and the economics for disposable income spending can directly affect the income revenue on your rental property. How do you hedge your bets for better results? Good question and I'll give you some of my tips and tricks, which may give you some results but are by no means a magic pill to solve every woe in a slow season.

Social Media Marketing Self-Help (The Ugly)

Hosts will have to take the time and invest in forms of social media marketing that puts their listings in front of as many potential guests as possible. This means thinking outside the box and not reliant on just AirBnB as your singular, rifle shot aim but rather a shot-gun approach, spreading your area of influence to hit as high a number of targets as possible and playing the percentages for bookings. How does this work exactly? This is where the time comes in for research and setting up various social media accounts to spread the message to a wider audience.

Research various vacation groups in your local area that have a Facebook Group page. We have quite a few, that go from Federal groups to Provincial groups to local group. In our area, there is hunting, ice fishing and summer fishing, bird watching groups, snow-shoeing groups, cross-country ski groups, snowmobile groups, etc. We even have a frisbee golf course locally that gets a lot of traffic. There are hiking groups to pickleball groups. Get on these groups and start reading the "looking for" postings. Put your link in the cut/copy/paste and make sure you have an easy to remember custom link on AirBnB. Make sure you read the ads so you know if this is a target guest and look for specifics, like the distance from they are looking for, if they have a pet, and specifics they list.

Keep in mind that it is not just the posting person who is reading the comments. Others will be reading the comments as well, so you are reaching a larger audience. The percentages of this may be low but there is the potential that you have ticked all the boxes for a repeat guest where you have satisfied the specific amenities they were wanting. Again, this is not scientific and requires time for you to do the research and respond.

Another method is to look at industry that hires contract workers and this includes your town and various building projects. Over the years we have been on various corporate HR department people simply by using a standard email introducing ourselves, our location and our accommodations links. This has also seen bookings in our otherwise, off-season, as corporations may not have the same requirements as vacationers looking for a sunny day at the beach.

We have also sent emails to insurance companies who are looking for a rental while a claimant needs to live during reconstruction or repairs. There are actually middle-men companies set up to find this for insurance companies and take a percentage of your percentage if you list with them. Like other host service sites, I'm a little skeptical at their results compared to their percentages and maybe their own hype. Maybe others can comment on their experiences.

Look at professional service industry contractors from a host of verticals, like entertainment, medical, agriculture, corporate offices, etc. where they may be looking for anything from STR to LTR for a specific time period.

Where is "The Good"?

Every investment of time and money should be towards an ROI (return on investment). Hopefully the comments and reviews left by the majority of guests gives you the ratings that other guests appreciate. Even on a negative review, if you use a combination of tactful diplomacy and humour this can go farther and create a more "humanistic word of mouth" advertising. I'll give you a case in point (real scenario) where we received three guests who read my response to a negative review and it made them laugh, so much so that they immediately chose to stay (and to specifically mention to me why they wanted to meet me as someone who shared their perspective).

Long story short, we had a drip coffee maker in the tiny house and provided coffee and filters for guests. We had guests who went on a rant about how bad the coffee was. My initial response was simple, "complimentary is not compulsory". The rest of my response was my decision to remove this from the tiny house in place of a Kuerig and guests can now bring their own coffee pucks and if they want to complain, then go ahead – your coffee, therefore, your fault. I inserted a little bit about maybe they never used a drip coffee maker and didn't know how much coffee to use (like one scoop per cup and one for the pot rule). My last point was to comment on how maybe they only know how to order a cup of coffee and leave it to the coffee barista to prepare for them.

AirBnB now has a policy where they will remove negative reviews where the host can prove that this was not accurate or simply retaliatory by the guest. Some guests have even held hosts hostage over wanting a price reduction or they would leave a negative review. This happens a lot more than you know. If the guest says they are a neophyte on AirBnB and would rather talk or text off-platform, explain that the communication stays on-platform to protect both host and guest equally. I've copied and pasted texts back into the AirBnB communication thread, so that any AirBnB Support Team person could read exactly what the guest wrote. In one case, this is instrumental in having the guest account removed from AirBnB for their threats. Long story that I may discuss in a podcast or livestream.

Anything that doesn't kill and you learn from, makes you stronger. Situations like this give you experience to refer to and increase your mettle.

SuperHost and what it really means. Being a SuperHost status is good and gives you a few perks but doing the extra work and attention to detail as a host is a lot for many people. The day we lost our superhost status, I was dumbfounded and felt personally hurt. The review was later removed and our status was reinstated but actually I remember reading a comment in an AirBnB Host Facebook group that made me look at this from a completely different perspective. When you stop trying to achieve the unachievable in pleasing everyone in every different request and scenario, it is actually a personally liberating experience.

Put simply, this meant I wasn't like a school student needing the A plus anymore on my report card. It took the stress off and allowed me to just relax and let things be as they are. This was a personal revelation for me to just provide the best I can and if this wasn't deserving for the guest rating, then the onus is half on them and not on me or what I did or didn't provide in their stay.

I've had guests say to me that this place was the best by far and they enjoyed their time immensely. Then I read their review and see their rating and, wow. No words. Once got a 3/5 on location and from the same person a 3/5 on pricing. Again, wow. First, you know where the place is when you book and everything is within walking distance. You know what you are paying in advance so is pricing subjective to what the guest felt they got in quality for their money? Also, some teachers who don't believe in a perfect score will go down the list and put 4/5 on every rating. Well, do the average and now your listing drops below the threshold of maintaining SuperHost status. My only advice, don't let the number rule your life. Do your best and let people do what they are going to do, regardless of the facts.

AirBnB now at least allows the Host to dispute a negative review, probably coming on the heels of knowing how guests are using this as leverage for either a better rate or a refund. This is why you keep all communications in writing on the platform. Guests will be very reluctant to put this coercive tactic in writing on the platform, knowing they can have their account suspended or removed permanently. I've read too many posts by hosts (poet and I know it) that have commented on this very fact.

My last point is not to live by the numbers or let them rule how you feel. This is not a good way to feel when you are always paranoid about not getting a good grade on your performance. Your hard work should be rewarded but for many reasons, it may not be. Personally, this hurts but you move past it and continue with your goals and let the chips fall where they may. I know this may not be the reassurance people are looking for, but it is the best that I can offer and the reality of most situations.

Thanks again for reading and let me know in the comments if there is any specific topic you wished discussed. Keep well.

Chapter Seven – Doing The Math

Preface of Marketing Principles

Any Host that relies one-hundred percent on just their AirBnB listing to draw in prospective guests is not living in the reality of the market. Having a listing on VRBO also aggregates to about fifty or so other sites, like hotels.com, Travelocity.com, etc and because of this, there are two middle-men payment percentages, which is why VRBO guests often pay a higher booking rate. Hosts have to understand that the listing is not the defacto only way to reach guests.

Understanding and using Social Media Marketing to their advantage, is how hosts are able to target local populations more likely to visit within the area just a short distance from their residence. These are more commonly phrased "Staycations". A confluence of factors caused the rise in reduced travel for vacations (due to Covid lockdowns) added to the inflation rates on energy pricing which hit the airlines and subsequently costs passed down to the traveler. If you are traveling on business, then no problem as it is not coming out of your pocket. For many others looking to vacation in their normal, pre-pandemic climate, this just wasn't possible.

Instead of seeing a decline in AirBnB guest bookings, there was actually a sharp increase. We can see that these are starting to decline back to pre-pandemic levels. Hosts should consider that they make themselves aware of not just the competition but other societal factors that are occurring in their markets that illustrate as "peaks and troughs" on demand. Simple things like an event or concert will drive up demand over a specific time period and something a host should pay attention to and monitor.

AirBnB Pricing Algorithm (Smart Pricing or Dumb Pricing?)

The "set it and forget it" of Smart Pricing employs a type of AI that is supposed to be doing comparative analysis in your local market of how many vacancies are remaining and at what price to reflect on your rates. In my personal experience, sometimes this works well and other times, it inflates the prices to an unrealistic amount for the reality of what guests are willing to pay. Case in point, when I had dynamic pricing on to try it out, it tripled my rate but there was really no justification in a comparative analysis. Maybe I was overthinking this problem but in the off season, many three season cottages are shut down over winter thereby reducing competition on the platform. With a limited number of listings coming up on a search, the Smart Pricing increased substantially, effectively pricing us out of the reality of the market.

This might be the "The Bad", where you should be getting bookings but potential guests are put-off by the higher than hotel rates being listed. Personally, I turned off the Smart Pricing feature and decided to, especially for the off-season rates, enter my own comparative rates with a little price comparison research. Not scientific or highly quantifiable but what I would expect to see as a guests searching for local accommodations. Having the history in the area to have seen the rates develop over the years gives me a little more insight than any AI algorithm just crunching numbers.

Some hosts may disagree and have seen amazing results from Smart Pricing. The only occurrence I can cite where this did work, was when there was a musical festival locally, with very high demand and low vacancy availability. In this one case our tiny house rented for about four times the normal rate over a week. Other than that, we have seen a decline in the bookings due to a number of factors, one of which is the dreaded off-season.

I should explain that the off-season of winter, still has a lot of activities and events which should see bookings. Depending on the year, word-of-mouth, the activities and the economics for disposable income spending can directly affect the income revenue on your rental property. How do you hedge your bets for better results? Good question and I'll give you some of my tips and tricks, which may give you some results but are by no means a magic pill to solve every woe in a slow season.

Social Media Marketing Self-Help (The Ugly)

Hosts will have to take the time and invest in forms of social media marketing that puts their listings in front of as many potential guests as possible. This means thinking outside the box and not reliant on just AirBnB as your singular, rifle shot aim but rather a shot-gun approach, spreading your area of influence to hit as high a number of targets as possible and playing the percentages for bookings. How does this work exactly? This is where the time comes in for research and setting up various social media accounts to spread the message to a wider audience.

Research various vacation groups in your local area that have a Facebook Group page. We have quite a few, that go from Federal groups to Provincial groups to local group. In our area, there is hunting, ice fishing and summer fishing, bird watching groups, snow-shoeing groups, cross-country ski groups, snowmobile groups, etc. We even have a frisbee golf course locally that gets a lot of traffic. There are hiking groups to pickleball groups. Get on these groups and start reading the "looking for" postings. Put your link in the cut/copy/paste and make sure you have an easy to remember custom link on AirBnB. Make sure you read the ads so you know if this is a target guest and look for specifics, like the distance from they are looking for, if they have a pet, and specifics they list.

Keep in mind that it is not just the posting person who is reading the comments. Others will be reading the comments as well, so you are reaching a larger audience. The percentages of this may be low but there is the potential that you have ticked all the boxes for a repeat guest where you have satisfied the specific amenities they were wanting. Again, this is not scientific and requires time for you to do the research and respond.

Another method is to look at industry that hires contract workers and this includes your town and various building projects. Over the years we have been on various corporate HR department people simply by using a standard email introducing ourselves, our location and our accommodations links. This has also seen bookings in our otherwise, off-season, as corporations may not have the same requirements as vacationers looking for a sunny day at the beach.

We have also sent emails to insurance companies who are looking for a rental while a claimant needs to live during reconstruction or repairs. There are actually middle-men companies set up to find this for insurance companies and take a percentage of your percentage if you list with them. Like other host service sites, I'm a little skeptical at their results compared to their percentages and maybe their own hype. Maybe others can comment on their experiences.

Look at professional service industry contractors from a host of verticals, like entertainment, medical, agriculture, corporate offices, etc. where they may be looking for anything from STR to LTR for a specific time period.

Where is "The Good"?

Every investment of time and money should be towards an ROI (return on investment). Hopefully the comments and reviews left by the majority of guests gives you the ratings that other guests appreciate. Even on a negative review, if you use a combination of tactful diplomacy and humour this can go farther and create a more "humanistic word of mouth" advertising. I'll give you a case in point (real scenario) where we received three guests who read my response to a negative review and it made them laugh, so much so that they immediately chose to stay (and to specifically mention to me why they wanted to meet me as someone who shared their perspective).

Long story short, we had a drip coffee maker in the tiny house and provided coffee and filters for guests. We had guests who went on a rant about how bad the coffee was. My initial response was simple, "complimentary is not compulsory". The rest of my response was my decision to remove this from the tiny house in place of a Kuerig and guests can now bring their own coffee pucks and if they want to complain, then go ahead – your coffee, therefore, your fault. I inserted a little bit about maybe they never used a drip coffee maker and didn't know how much coffee to use (like one scoop per cup and one for the pot rule). My last point was to comment on how maybe they only know how to order a cup of coffee and leave it to the coffee barista to prepare for them.

AirBnB now has a policy where they will remove negative reviews where the host can prove that this was not accurate or simply retaliatory by the guest. Some guests have even held hosts hostage over wanting a price reduction or they would leave a negative review. This happens a lot more than you know. If the guest says they are a neophyte on AirBnB and would rather talk or text off-platform, explain that the communication stays on-platform to protect both host and guest equally. I've copied and pasted texts back into the AirBnB communication thread, so that any AirBnB Support Team person could read exactly what the guest wrote. In one case, this is instrumental in having the guest account removed from AirBnB for their threats. Long story that I may discuss in a podcast or livestream. Anything that doesn't kill and you learn from, makes you stronger. Situations like this give you experience to refer to and increase your mettle.

SuperHost and what it really means. Being a SuperHost status is good and gives you a few perks but doing the extra work and attention to detail as a host is a lot for many people. The day we lost our superhost status, I was dumbfounded and felt personally hurt. The review was later removed and our status was reinstated but actually I remember reading a comment in an AirBnB Host Facebook group that made me look at this from a completely different perspective. When you stop trying to achieve the unachievable in pleasing everyone in every different request and scenario, it is actually a personally liberating experience.

Put simply, this meant I wasn't like a school student needing the A plus anymore on my report card. It took the stress off and allowed me to just relax and let things be as they are. This was a personal revelation for me to just provide the best I can and if this wasn't deserving for the guest rating, then the onus is half on them and not on me or what I did or didn't provide in their stay.

I've had guests say to me that this place was the best by far and they enjoyed their time immensely. Then I read their review and see their rating and, wow. No words. Once got a 3/5 on location and from the same person a 3/5 on pricing. Again, wow. First, you know where the place is when you book and everything is within walking distance. You know what you are paying in advance so is pricing subjective to what the guest felt they got in quality for their money? Also, some teachers who don't believe in a perfect score will go down the list and put 4/5 on every rating. Well, do the average and now your listing drops below the threshold of maintaining SuperHost status. My only advice, don't let the number rule your life. Do your best and let people do what they are going to do, regardless of the facts.

AirBnB now at least allows the Host to dispute a negative review, probably coming on the heels of knowing how guests are using this as leverage for either a better rate or a refund. This is why you keep all communications in writing on the platform. Guests will be very reluctant to put this coercive tactic in writing on the platform, knowing they can have their account suspended or removed permanently. I've read too many posts by hosts (poet and I know it) that have commented on this very fact.

My last point is not to live by the numbers or let them rule how you feel. This is not a good way to feel when you are always paranoid about not getting a good grade on your performance. Your hard work should be rewarded but for many reasons, it may not be. Personally, this hurts but you move past it and continue with your goals and let the chips fall where they may. I know this may not be the reassurance people are looking for, but it is the best that I can offer and the reality of most situations.

Thanks again for reading and let me know in the comments if there is any specific topic you wished discussed. Keep well.

Chapter Eight – Protecting Your Investment

Attracting the Guest you want.

Your rental property is your investment and should be protected. If you have created a space for a particular type of rental clientele, then everything you do should be tailored to that person. Many radio stations have use a composite picture in the booth to remind the disc jockey who they are speaking to, as the customer or listener of their station. Hosts should be doing the same and identifying the composite of the customer they are looking to attract. If this is the not clients you are getting, then something needs work to correct this.

The theme you present to the guests in your property could be an indicator of the kind of client you are looking to attract. The pictures you use and how they communicate visually the property and the surroundings they will enjoy. This includes the driveway area for parking – ie. Are your guests bringing a boat to do fishing? If so, make sure this is part of your advertising that might be the defining factor in their decision to rent your property over others being offered. Same goes for making your property "pet friendly" as many properties are not set up for this. List the items and amenities that defines your property from your competition in the area. As a quick note, if we do have anyone doing fishing (boat or ice fishing) we ask that they not use our kitchen for cleaning their catch. Just a friendly reminder and believe me, if they want to book your place in future trips, they will abide by your request without worry.

Pricing as a Marketing Strategy

Many times the guest who contacts you looking for a "deal" on the price is not the guest you want at your property. Never be the most expensive but never be the cheapest. Price is a strategy used to target the upper end of the clients you want to stay at your property. We don't use a damage deposit as we know the property is insured and also covered by AirBnB resolutions for any specific damages (within 14 days of the booking check out date). You are looking for the guest who is going to respect your property and treat it like they would their own house.

Targeting the pricing strategy that becomes a type of filter to dissuade the guest you don't want from wanting to book your property. Some may read this as being "elitist". Not so. Tiffany's doesn't compete with WalMart and are targeting their clientele in everything they do and how they present themselves. This is marketing and knowing your customer so you can target and communicate, advertise, directly to them. We'll talk more about pricing strategies when we look over the projection spreadsheets.

We have hosted some guests who have no issue with the rental rates considering the type of vehicles they drive and equipment they own. Some have boats worth more than the brand new trucks they have hauling them. For them, to spend a few extra dollars to know they are in a safe area, with security cameras, etc means they have peace of mind and that has a quantifiable value.

Asking the Right Questions – Qualifying the Customer

For years I would lecture to my students on having the ability to "qualify the customer". This means asking questions and listening to the responses in order to evaluate (qualitatively in most cases), what they are looking for and if you can provide what they need. If you can't, then it may be hard to say, but "no" is a perfectly acceptable response in business. Many times we've had inquiries that sent up some warning signals. In most cases, it was a calculation of risk versus reward. What is the cost if this guest damages my property (my investment) that it is not available for the next guests?

Part of my research is being "plugged in" on social media groups of other hosts to read about their "misfortunes" from a recent guest experience. If it is in your area, don't hold back on sending a DM to the person who posted asking for a name or to confirm a name of a person who inquired at your property. This group resource is a form of "word of mouth" protection of your investment.

Number one red flag is someone who lives in the area looking to book your place. If they are looking at a weekend that happens to be when a major sporting playoff happens to be occurring, this should be a cautionary flag for sure. Ask why, if they live in the area, are they wanting to book your place. I've had people ask to book just one night (and we have a two-night minimum). This is a red flag for using your property as a "party house". Our rules are zero tolerance on two things: no smoking inside property and no parties.

If my camera comes up with multiple cars and multiple people, more than were originally in the booking, then I immediately communicate on the platform via message that the guests must leave the property by 11pm, as only those guests who are registered are insured and there is a sound bylaw from 11pm to 8am.

With our Nest Camera's and the ability to record video segments, if there is something going on, then it is dealt with immediately. If you have alerts going off after 11pm, then you can send a reminder (polite and tactful warning). If it continues then it is dealt with immediately, reminding the guest that violation of the rules means they can be evicted from the property immediately. I've only had to do this (fortunately) very few times but it has been more prevalent in recent years with changes to AirBnB policies.

As an example, I have "instant booking" enabled and it has worked fine until recently. My understanding was that anyone with a new profile without any trips is unable to use the instant booking option. This must have changed, as we had a guest who booked, same day (literally in the afternoon of the check-in date). My questions to AirBnB are still unanswered on how this could be allowed. The notifications were going off and I messaged the guest twice, before finally at 3am informing them that they had violated our policy (no smoking and noise) and they should pack their things and I would be there in minutes to escort them off the property. When I got there, it was not good. Suffice it to say, they were there to party the weekend away without any care for the property. They had to call a cab (so they didn't even have a car) to get back to the city.

On a cursory inspection, there was damage and missing items, burnt matches everywhere, etc. The guests was insistent they were not smoking even with physical evidence to the contrary. A simple gesture to my phone and asking if she wanted me to send her the video of people coming from the house smoking? The investment of the cameras are a necessity in these types of situations, as the footage doesn't lie.

Questions, Questions, Questions.

Ask as many inquiry questions as you need in order to satisfy your concerns. Make sure the communications are on the platform and if they want to communicate over the phone or via text, persuade them to keep all communications on the AirBnB Messages. This should be a warning sign and believe me, I've had people claim "I'm a neophyte on AirBnB" – don't believe it. I even cut/copied and pasted text messages back into the AirBnB Message so that the communication thread could be seen by the AirBnB Support people. Take screenshots of text messages and always refer back to communicating on the platform. This is not only the AirBnB rules, but it is protection for both you and the guest in case of any dispute or mediation required later. If the guest has used abusive or coercive language, this violates the AirBnB policy off the hop. Any resolution person who reads this should immediately get a clear picture of the guest and make arrangements for them to be removed from the platform.

What is the purpose of your stay? Can you confirm how many people in your group and the age groups? How many vehicles? Any special requirement for their stay? Based on the responses, you may have some follow-up questions to ask. You don't have to be annoying but the more information you receive the better you can evaluate the Pre-Approval acceptance. Don't forget that even after you accept, the guest has 48 hours to verify the booking, so that this is their responsibility. I've had the odd occasion where someone instantly booked dates where the guest had not confirmed and accepted the reservation. This happens, so I make them aware that those dates remain available on the calendar until they have booked and locked-in the dates.

We can continue with various scenarios of how to qualify the customer properly. Since I have my Keynote Presentation on this, I will organize a moderated Zoom online chat and go through all the questions. If there are any inconsistencies in the responses you get, this should raise a cautionary flag in your mind and allows you to ask further questions to clarify these concerns.

Most are good, honest people but every so often there is a bad element that you want to steer clear of. Your investment is not worth the risk and I have turned down multiple week reservations when these types of issues and concerns overshadowed the booking. Don't allow your short-term greed to get a booking blind you to the potential hazards of having to repair and the time for making claims on a dispute is a hassle you don't need.

Learn from others and their experience so you don't have to. That is the central theme of why I am writing this in the first place. Keep well and safe.

Chapter Nine – Estimates and Spreadsheets

Running the Numbers

	A	B	C	D	E	F	G
1	Rent ROI Estimates for AirBnB/VRBO Options						
2							
3	rates/nights	2	3	4	5	6	7
4	$135.00	$270.00	$405.00	$540.00	$675.00	$810.00	$945.00
5	$140.00	$280.00	$420.00	$560.00	$700.00	$840.00	$980.00
6	$145.00	$290.00	$435.00	$580.00	$725.00	$870.00	$1,015.00
7	$150.00	$300.00	$450.00	$600.00	$750.00	$900.00	$1,050.00
8	$155.00	$310.00	$465.00	$620.00	$775.00	$930.00	$1,085.00
9	$160.00	$320.00	$480.00	$640.00	$800.00	$960.00	$1,120.00
10	$165.00	$330.00	$495.00	$660.00	$825.00	$990.00	$1,155.00
11	$170.00	$340.00	$510.00	$680.00	$850.00	$1,020.00	$1,190.00
12	$175.00	$350.00	$525.00	$700.00	$875.00	$1,050.00	$1,225.00
13							
14	Days	25%	30%	40%	50%	60%	75%
15	365	91	110	146	183	219	274
16							
17	$135.00	$12,318.75	$14,782.50	$19,710.00	$24,637.50	$29,565.00	$36,956.25
18	$140.00	$12,775.00	$15,330.00	$20,440.00	$25,550.00	$30,660.00	$38,325.00
19	$145.00	$13,231.25	$15,877.50	$21,170.00	$26,462.50	$31,755.00	$39,693.75
20	$150.00	$13,687.50	$16,425.00	$21,900.00	$28,287.50	$32,850.00	$41,062.50
21	$155.00	$14,143.75	$16,972.50	$22,630.00	$28,287.50	$33,945.00	$42,431.25
22	$160.00	$14,600.00	$17,520.00	$23,360.00	$30,112.50	$35,040.00	$43,800.00
23	$165.00	$15,056.25	$18,067.50	$24,090.00	$30,112.50	$36,135.00	$45,168.75
24	$170.00	$15,512.50	$18,615.00	$24,820.00	$31,025.00	$37,230.00	$46,537.50
25	$175.00	$15,968.75	$19,162.50	$25,550.00	$31,937.50	$38,325.00	$47,906.25

Above is a screenshot showing the spreadsheet that I created as a planning tool. I use this in combination with my other spreadsheets on my expenses (fixed and variable) along with my loan and mortgage information. Just a quick note before we get into the details and mechanics of how this works and that is knowing your payment terms with your bank. What you want to find out is how many years your mortgage is amortized over. Obviously the longer the term, the more interest you are paying on whatever money you borrow. What you want is a "financially comfortable" repayment plan that limits the amount of interest you are paying. The more you do this, the more money you will save from paying out in fees and interest. Also, find out from them about lump sum payments on the principal amount and options for accelerated payments. Lump sum payment is usually 15% of the principal amount can be paid down without penalty. That the is the original principal amount you borrowed, so put simply, if that was $100,000 dollars, then you can pay $15,000 each calendar year, reducing your interest payments substantially.

On the accelerated payments, instead of paying once a month, if you pay the same amount every week instead, you actually reduce the principal amount faster and this could mean a savings of thousands over the term of the loan or mortgage. Many people don't take the time to investigate all these options and depending on your bank-person, they may not offer the information and just put you into a boilerplate loan or mortgage. By knowing your payment options and how you can benefit is worth setting up a meeting and asking questions (doing research).

The sooner you have paid down your investment, the sooner your Return On Investment (ROI) and owning the property along with all proceeds from your rental. Also, your equity in the property is completely unencumbered meaning that you can use this property as leverage to purchase another property. As long as the real estate market is healthy, any bank or lender will ascribe a valuation on the property and allow you to borrow a Home Equity Line of Credit (HELOC) that is usually up to a 70% valuation. Keep this in mind that you now have equity that you can use if a property comes available that allows you to build your rental portfolio.

Mechanics of the Spreadsheet

If we review the spreadsheet, what you will see is the one on top is broken down with the first vertical column indicating the rate or amount per night, multiplied by the top horizontal row indicating the number of nights (starting with a minimum two-night stay). You can adjust your rate and it will ripple through the other fields in the spreadsheet doing your calculations across the board for you. This way you can try various minimum and maximum ranges, perhaps for peak season and off-season rates.

The highlighted line is my median rate that is my minimum target rate. I use this for the off-season rates as my minimum benchmark. Once we've established our high and low benchmarks, we can then extrapolate this to figure out a realistic vacancy rate. Will your place be booked every day of a year for 365 days? Most likely not, so what you want to do is have a realistic evaluation of your vacancy rates from 25%, 50% and 75% (and higher or lower if you want). By allowing the spreadsheet to do the calculations, you can determine your worst case and best-case scenario. The technology is merely a tool in helping you to plan.

Breakeven Point – Knowing Fixed and Variable Expenses

You can easily build a spreadsheet that itemizes your expenses along with estimating your income potential to find your "financial comfort zone" or what the banks refer to as the "financial stress test". Can you afford the mortgage payments? Can you afford the carry cost on the property? This includes some expenses that will be annually paid, like the home owner's insurance and the property taxes.

Make your list of utility expenses, some will be monthly and depending on where you live, some may be quarterly. Know the frequency and the amounts, as best you can to populate your spreadsheet accurately. Account for increases year over year for inflationary cost of living increases, any additional taxes that may be levied in the future, etc. Being very conservative in your estimations, you may also want to add a 10% to 15% contingency factor. This contingency factor budgets for unforeseen circumstances that may arise during the course of the year.

Some businesses refer to the term "spillage" for the unforeseen loss they might have on their revenue. In your case it could be an increase in your insurance premium or a repair that needs to be done in order to upkeep your property. Remember, the property is your investment and must be maintained in order that guests are comfortable for their stay. If the water heater is old, then budget a "building fund" to put money aside from your profits that will be used to re-invest in the upgrades to your property.

If you just "take the money and run" and turn your back on the investment, then just like a car it will depreciate in value and eventually breakdown. Make sure you don't fall into this trap. Please remember, any dollar of investment in your property is an equity investment. If you sell later down the road, then you can prove to any potential buyer that the property has been properly serviced and maintained (just like selling a car and showing all the service orders and invoices).

If you are looking at purchasing a property then you will want to pull all the receipts for all the utilities expenses, property taxes, insurance premiums and any and all repairs and maintenance done (some may have transferable warranties that you inherit as the new owner, which could save you thousands potentially for having this paperwork in place). As this is a large investment, hire a home inspection company that will go through the property to itemize all the "good, bad and ugly". They will hopefully give you some insight on your purchase and any things you may have to consider repairing or upgrading when you purchase.

Small item but one worth mentioning – ask if there is a survey of the land that the property is situated on. If there is not, you may want for many reasons to request one from the seller (at their cost) to assure that there is no issues with any neighbouring properties or property owners. This actually happened recently and is why I am flagging this for you, to save you money and time dealing with a neighbour that might not be "neighbourly". Just a consideration to be aware of as this could cost thousands to resolve any property line dispute in future.

Geotechnical Reports

Another point to consider if you are purchasing a property that potentially could be on a fault line or slope of some kind. This has come up as well when we were putting out for tender for insurance quotes. Some companies are now requiring this as part of them providing insurance for your property. Getting this report may cost multiple thousands of dollars, so be very careful and have this as a point of consideration when purchasing. Talk to insurance brokers and have them make sure (and if possible, give you a written waiver that this will not be a requirement) that this is not a condition of their coverage.

Amenities and ROI

I've seen ads by potential rental customers asking for a pool, hot tub, outdoor fireplace, etc. In my opinion, you provide amenities that are low maintenance and therefore low cost but important for the customer to enjoy their stay. These would be outside seating, patio table dining area, a BBQ (I prefer natural gas to not have to deal with exchange of propane tanks) and a fireplace area. Hot tubs and pools are great but they are costly to purchase and even more to maintain properly. In addition to the running costs of these items, there is also the liability to consider while you are operating these amenities available to guests. This will most certainly increase your insurance premiums for liability. Another point, it reduces your ROI and increases the time before your breakeven is met. It also doesn't really add any equity value to your property and you have to charge more per guest stay to recoup your costs, therefore pushing your rates maybe above the general range of most people.

We are fortunate, as we have a lake where guests can swim and enjoy all kinds of water sports and activities. We have a hot tub that didn't get used for many summers even though we thought we would. If you keep in mind and focus on "why is your customer booking?" then extra amenities may not be what they are wanting. If they are in town for an event like a wedding or on business, these extra amenities are a "nice to have but not a need to have". As a guest if they would rather pay an extra $50 per night for a hot tub? Then calculate the purchase price, the install price (plumbing, electrical, and building a deck or platform, etc) and you will find your ROI is over years, while it depreciates in value on the resale market. Just look at used hot tubs and you will find that there are some marked "free". Why is this? Probably my guess, it got old and the owners found it more work and cost for what they used it.

Always remember, this is not your house that you are living in. This is a rental property and what you may want is not a concern for anyone wanting to rent on a short-term basis. Many times, we had to remind ourselves of this fact. Is a guest going to pay extra per night for… and you fill in the blank. If the answer is "no", then it is a simple decision. I've had this conversation regarding buying kayaks, canoes, golf carts, etc. Most guests bring what they want to use, like bikes, boats, etc. and you providing these adds a liability issue if you don't provide the proper equipment and in some cases training.

Chapter Ten – Marketing Local and WOM

Target Marketing

We've talked a little about target marketing and utilizing social media Facebook Groups as a means of spreading the word to potential guests. If you are like me, you set up a system with cut/copy/paste information, links, etc. This will mitigate your time on task and make you much more efficient when it comes time to responding to inquiries and posting comments with links. Many times, I will review various posts for people looking for a place to rent. Read them over carefully and even if my listing doesn't tick all the boxes, I still post a comment with the link, as the consideration for them to make a decision could be any number of conditions or factors.

Realistically, a customer decision could come down to distance traveled, cost, amenities versus the amenities on their "wish list". Also, don't forget that your exposure is not just to the person who posted the request but also for other vacationers (or potential vacationers) who might be scrolling through. This is why I always comment publicly on the post instead of doing a DM (Direct Message). When viewing other listings in your area, try and do the SWOT Analysis (strengths, weaknesses, opportunities, threats). This is a quick overview of what your competition may be offering their guests that compares to your listing(s). As I'm typing this, I'm still eagerly awaiting the AirBnB App update that has promised to do this analysis comparison for you.

One of the main items we noted was that there was not as many "pet friendly" accommodations. This is necessary for people traveling with a pet or who don't wish to board their pet during their vacation. By pre-planning your property and providing the necessary features, like food bowls, pooper scooper bags, kitty litter box, etc. the number of potential guests increases. Also, your property is flagged in direct search queries where they have selected "pet friendly". We add a nominal per stay or per night fee that covers maybe some additional cleaning required. All our flooring (except for one room) is done specifically as vinyl or wood, so the probability of damage is greatly reduced or mitigated.

Local Business to Business Marketing

On the topic of pet friendly accommodations for our guests, we also have an arrangement with a local supplier of all natural dog treats. We make sure that there is a complimentary bag, which advertises their brand which is available to our guests at the local Farmer's Market. This is an amenity for the furry member of the family and much appreciated by the guests. This also promotes local business and there is a complimentary effect of them promoting your properties to their customers. This creates a support of local business along with a win/win/win; you benefit, the local business benefits and the guests benefit.

Look for these opportunities. We promote local business whenever we get the opportunity. Our local business association created a "business map" outlining the area along with an advertising for all the businesses that contributed to the printing of the map. These maps are placed in all our properties and we encourage visitors to keep them, share them, etc. We talk to all our local businesses, including our (perceived) competition. Many times, I've referred inquiries to our local motel when we were booked. It took a bit but the effort was soon reciprocated when I received an inquiry that started with "we were talking to … and they told us to give you a call…".

Karma is a cyclical pattern of cause and effect. You put out good vibes and stay true and you are sure the same will reflect back. We now do this for a number of home-based businesses, where they provide home cooked meals and desserts. We also provide a gift certificate to our guests to a local restaurant that has amazing meals, treats and home-made ice cream (Death By Chocolate being my personal favourite). I may sound "old school" when I say this, but keep your rolodex expanding and make sure you are supporting local business. Keep in mind the adage of having more than one supplier in business, so you have a contingency. In most cases, this could be a game-changer when it comes time to helping you in a situation that arises that might have been unexpected.

WOM

Word-of-Mouth. The advertising that doesn't cost you monetarily and provides the seal of approval directly from someone else. Along this line, it is great when a personal passion intersects with this ethos. Here is my real-life example that guests really appreciate. We support the local cat rescue non-profit organization with various donations, that guests help us to support. Firstly, it started with us donating for a silent auction fundraiser to a different non-profit group fundraising for a seeing eye dog. Again, the call came from a word-of-mouth referral. We happily donated each year and many of the winning bidders stayed with us only to become annual booking guests. We expanded this to the cat rescue fundraising nights with great success.

It doesn't stop there. We also let guests know that all our recycling goes to the cat rescue for their fundraising efforts. Guests love that they know they are in a small way, helping to contribute to these local efforts. But it doesn't stop there. We had an assortment of books that I would buy at garage sales for something the guest could do during a rainy day when the beach is not amenable due to weather. Guests could also take the book to read at the beach on a sunny day. Either way, it is was something we provided to all our guests, like playing cards, games, etc. for them to enjoy during their stay. By accident, one of our guests left a note saying that they started a book and wanted to finish it, so they left a five-dollar bill to pay for the book. This was a surprise and an opportunity to raise more money for the cat rescue.

We immediately informed the guest that their money would be donated and thanked them for leaving it. Now we have a donation box with a note, "take a book and help support our local non-profit cat rescue". Now people at garage sales are calling me to pick up boxes of books they have for our in-property selection of books for guests. Rather than sell their books for pennies, they call me to take the boxes and "pay it forward". This was completely accidental but has now become yet another amenity that we provide that benefits others. Making these donations are great and helping to support a worthwhile cause has created copy-cat (no pun intended) scenarios and we couldn't be happier to hear this.

Also never forget that your guests are connected via social media. Many have taken pictures and posted glowing vacation testimonial posts that have shown people not only where they were staying but also all the great things about coming here to visit for anyone considering a vacation in the future. This is social media word-of-mouth where I don't have Instagram, yet our tiny house has been featured prominently by our guests. No time or cost to me and this direct recommendation is overly beneficial to all your goals. We also have post cards of the tiny house that guests can take and share with friends, as just a physical means of advertising.

If the adage of you have to remind the customer at least seven times before they commit to making a purchase, all these combined makes sure your message is being sent and resent and resent until it moves through the ether to your next potential guests.

Competition Versus Self-Competition

In our particular area, there was not much opportunity to rent. We were the first to provide an STR alternative to renting a cottage by the month, and most of those were year over year with a wait-list of rental guests. Waiting for someone to drop off the wait-list was probably frustrating. We were surprised by the reception we received and our ROI was initially over five years and we did that it under three years. There was a learning curve and factoring all the various facets of creating a worthwhile guest experience.

Opening in summer 2024 is a brand new six-unit motel for our local township. Many have said, aren't you worried. To the contrary. This will provide a barometer to guests to see what they get for their money. If this fits with their plans, no problem. We see it as a place to refer guests who are sitting on the fence and let them do the comparisons. If this place is busy that means that we will also be busy catering to the guests who don't fit the customer profile of this motel. Is it pet friendly? Are they providing a full kitchen? Are they offering an outdoor fireplace area? Are they offering a private space for their family and friends to enjoy? There is a major difference between a whole home rental compared to a one-room motel room stay. We hope they are successful as success breeds success, even if it is for your competition (which may not entirely be your competition).

Our hope is that we stay in touch with these owners and they become our friends in supporting local.

Are you asking the right questions?

Over the last few months, I've read a number of posts where the rentals have been "flat". This could be a symptom of the times we live, with less disposable income as the cost-of-living increases across the board. This is why every host must be aware of the market, their competition, their rates, their amenities, their community, etc. Being online is not simply a "set it and forget it" proposition. There is time you need to devote in order to do the necessary tweaks and changes as they are required. Try things and see how the changes work or not, and ask yourself "why" or what you could do differently. In order to get the result, you cannot be prescriptive in what you think you need. You might have to reframe the question and be more analytical in your approach.

Seeing most of the rental posts asking for advice when they look great and have very positive reviews means they have to look at the market conditions (location, location, location – could be a factor) or their pricing strategy. If inflation continues it means simply that the value of your spending dollar is now lower than it was the day before. There is also a corollary effect that most people never consider (and again depends on the market conditions and location) but your investment should be gaining equity even if the property sits empty.

Reframing might be a difficult task if you are in the forest and can't see the trees. You could have friends or relatives stay at your place for a few nights and give you their honest opinions on what you might want to do in order to make improvements for your guests. Stay at your property yourself and try to see it as if you were a guest staying there. Maybe stay at a competitors' property or read their reviews to see what guests are commenting on.

As a last point, I find it surprising to me that most groups on Facebook that claim to be there for "hosts to help other hosts" and allow people to post (advertise) their listings are hypocritical and won't allow me to post links for people to read my eBook or offer suggestions on topics. It is what it is and they have their reasons but have not been given one that defies their mission statements. This is my rant for today and will leave it there. Happy holidays to everyone who has made it this far in the reading. If you want to let me know what you think or topics for consideration, please let me know. Keep well and all the best for 2024.

If you enjoyed these chapters, there will be a second volume which explores the aspects of creating templates for an automated Property Management template. How to use a slow Real-Estate Market to entice property owners on the benefits of STR (short-term rental) or LTR (long-term rental). Thank you and hope your journey is as pleasant and profitable as ours has been.

www.ingramcontent.com/pod-product-compliance
Lightning Source LLC
Chambersburg PA
CBHW070417230526
45471CB00006B/2858